POM POM
ANIMALS

Project Book

Learn how to make a collection
of pom pom animals

10 projects inside

2

INTRODUCTION

Pom pom animals are fun and easy to make. These adorable fluffy creatures are made by wrapping yarn into pom poms. Then with a bit of delicate trimming, shaping and creativity, these little animals come to life!

There are so many animals you can create with very little imagination.

We have included all the components to make two adorable little bears, to start your new pom pom family. But don't stop there, we have also provided lots more patterns, including bunnies, pandas, lions, birds and more.

Whether they're bundled in a basket or hung on a ribbon, these cute, furry creatures are adored by everyone. They are the perfect gift and their beautiful cute faces make them irresistible.

Let's get started!

KIT CONTENTS

WHAT'S INCLUDED:

Pom Pom Maker (Medium)
Brown Yarn 25g (per bear)
Black Yarn 10g (per bear)
Plastic Eyes
Felting Needle
Waxed thread

WHAT YOU'LL NEED:

Sharp Scissors
Craft Glue

To get started, we would recommend reading over the introductions and key technique tips. Once you have done this, it's time to move onto the "bear" project and get going with your animal pom pom makes. Let the fun begin!

POM POM MAKING BASICS

All these adorable pom poms start life by wrapping yarn around a pom pom maker.

- There are different sizes of pom pom maker. In this book, our patterns are all based on a medium size, as provided in your kit

- The size of your final pom pom can be adapted by wrapping a little less or more yarn around your maker

- For these animals, we have provided DK Yarn and suggest you use this for all other makes. This provides the best texture and gives them their fluffy and adorable faces

- To tie your pom pom together, you can simply use a piece of yarn, or if you want a tighter hold, you can use waxed thread – or even something around the house like dental floss works just as well

- Don't be concerned if your animal pom pom doesn't start off looking as cute as you may have hoped for, the secret lies in the trimming!

- With trimming, you must be brave; use the pattern guides provided to develop the animals shape. Keep trimming into shape and you will start to see your animal come to life

- You will need a total of around 40-50g of yarn for each pom pom animal you make. This may be divided into different colours, for example you may need around 90% of the colour of yarn used for their body and then 10% will be in the colours chosen for eyes, ears and nose. Be sure to calculate the approximate yarn required before starting any of these projects

THE BASICS:

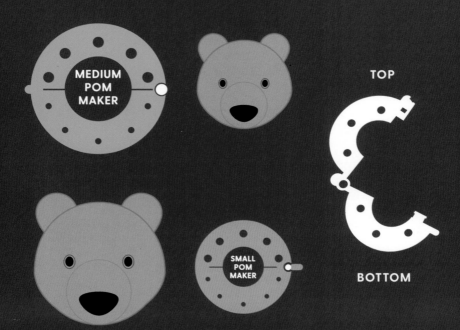

MEDIUM POM MAKER

SMALL POM MAKER

TOP

BOTTOM

8

HOW TO NEEDLE FELT

Be careful! The needle is very sharp. It is always best to use a thimble and foam sponge to felt against where possible.

NOSE

Gather the yarn around the nose to create a snout. Then begin to needle felt until the yarn holds together and keeps its shape.

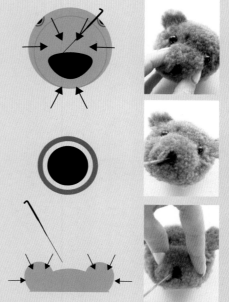

EYES

Needle felt the black yarn (the eyes) until they are rounded and stay in place. Once happy, you can stick your plastic eyes, provided in your kit, on top of the yarn with craft glue.

EARS

For each ear, hold the yarn together before slowly needle felting. Do this until the ear stays in shape and the yarn is bonded. Then, cut into a rounded ear shape as shown in the diagram.

TOP TIP:
Facial features can be defined by continuing to needle felt around nose and eyes. You can refine your bear with more trimming until you are happy with the shape.

MAKES 2   50 MINS
PER MAKE

MAKE
WITH KIT
CONTENTS!

BARLEY
THE BEAR

BEAR (MAKES 2)

Before you start, get everything you need laid out and ready to use. Make sure to divide the black and brown yarn in half at this stage – put half to one side ready for your second bear make. You will want to start by picking up your pom pom maker; making sure the hinge is on the left-hand side. Open the maker ready to start wrapping the yarn around the top half. Each stage positions and layers the yarn in place to create the animal's facial features, so make sure you copy the pattern precisely and remember which half is the top of the head.

Keep on trimming your pom pom to get the perfect bear!

YOU WILL NEED

- Pom Pom Maker (Medium)
- Brown Yarn 25g (per bear)
- Black Yarn 10g (per bear)
- Eyes
- Felting Needle
- Waxed thread

KIT CONTENTS

- Sharp Scissors
- Craft Glue

METHOD

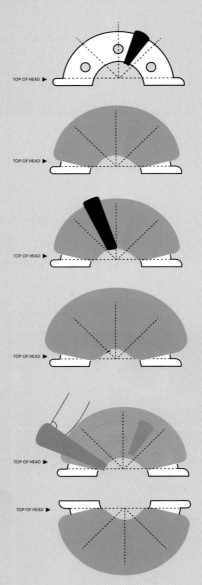

1 THE NOSE

Wrap the black yarn around your marker 12 times, in the postion shown.

2 THE HEAD

Next, wrap the brown yarn from left to right, over the top of the nose approx. 200 wraps. This will create 3-4 layers over the entire maker.

3 THE EYES

Now you want to use the black yarn again, wrapping 10 times in the position shown.

4 THE HEAD CONTINUED

Continue to wrap the brown yarn around the pom pom maker until it is completely full. The thicker you wrap, the fluffier the pom pom will be.

5 THE EARS

Place your finger in the position shown and wrap brown yarn over your finger and the maker 12 times. Make sure you wrap on the 'top of head'.

STEPS FOR THE BOTTOM HALF

6 SECOND HALF

Making sure you are on the bottom half of the maker, begin to wrap the brown yarn from left to right until it is fully covered. Around 230 wraps.

BRING IT TOGETHER

Bring the two halves of the pom pom maker together and join using the clip.

STEPS FOR CUTTING AND TYING

CUTTING

Hold the closed maker together and turn to the side. Use small, sharp scissors to cut in-between each side of the maker, as shown.

TYING

Use your waxed thread and wrap around the centre twice, before tying and pulling a tight knot. To be fully secure repeat with a second knot.

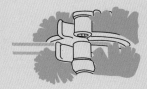

TRIMMING

Once you have your scissors, begin trimming your bear pom pom into shape, as shown in the diagrams. Pay careful attention to the curve of the nose and cheeks. Be patient and just keep trimming, it will not look right at first!

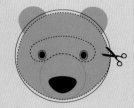

1 THE EYES

Trim around the eyes as shown. You will need to shorten the pom pom in this eye area to form the face, making sure to keep the nose longer and accenuate it.

2 THE HEAD

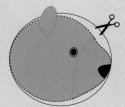

Shape the head as shown in the diagram. Do not cut the ears at this stage!

3 THE SIDE

Cut at the side angle to get the shape shown – particularly focusing on the curve around the nose and eyes.

Lastly, continue trimming and neatening until you get the desired look for your pom pom animal. Keep turning to check the animals shape looks right from all sides.

NEEDLE FELTING

Nose

Gather the yarn around the nose to create a snout. Then begin to needle felt until the yarn holds together and keeps its shape.

Eyes

Needle felt the black yarn (the eyes) until they are rounded and stay in place. Once happy, you can stick the plastic eyes, provided in your kit, on top of the yarn with craft glue.

Ears

For each ear, hold the yarn together before slowly needle felting. Do this until the ear stays in shape and the yarn is bonded. Then, cut into a rounded ear shape as shown in the diagram.

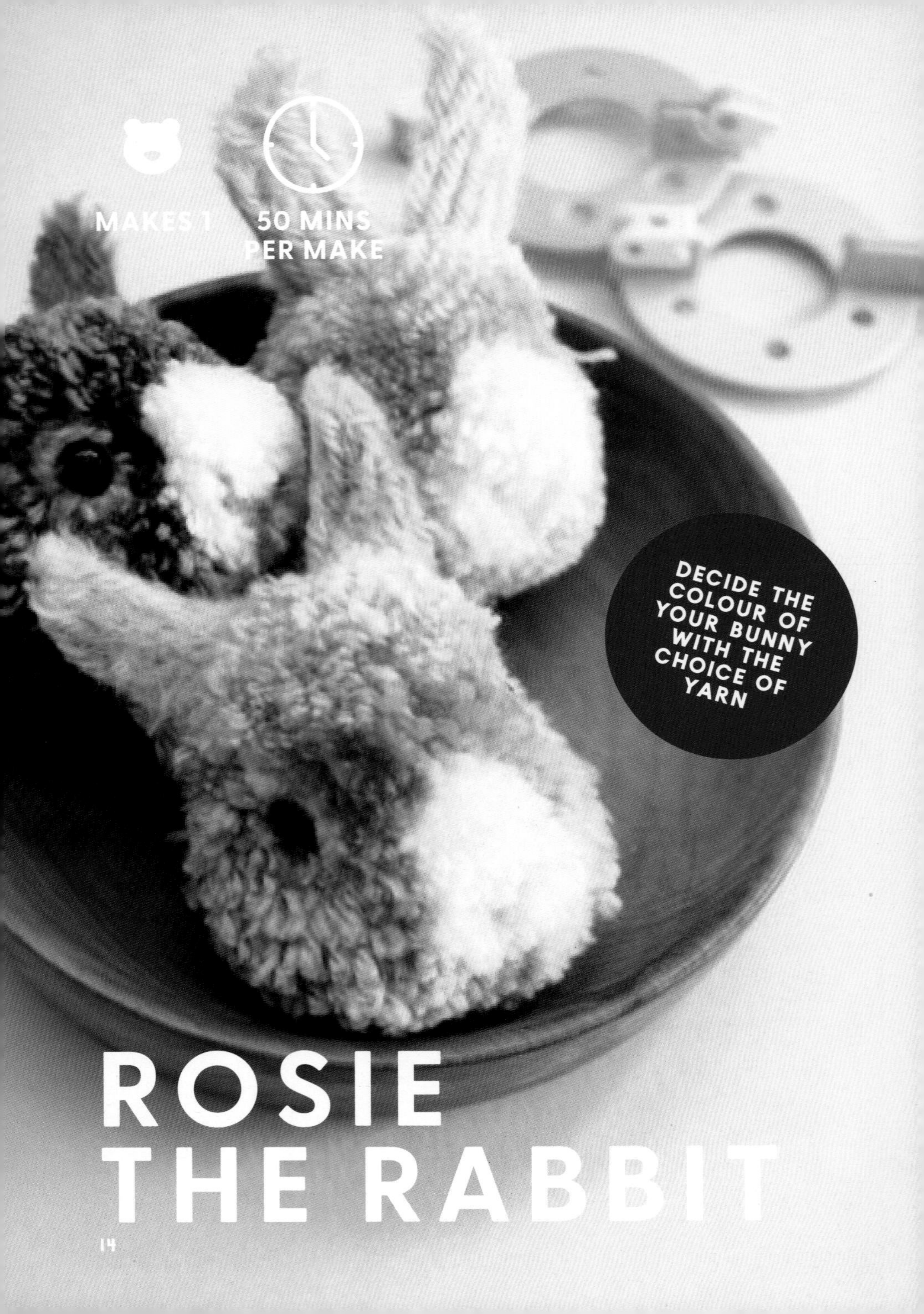

MAKES 1

50 MINS
PER MAKE

DECIDE THE
COLOUR OF
YOUR BUNNY
WITH THE
CHOICE OF
YARN

ROSIE
THE RABBIT

RABBIT

YOU WILL NEED

· Pom Pom Maker (Medium)
· Pink Yarn
· White Yarn
· Brown or Grey Yarn
· Plastic Eyes (optional)
· Waxed Thread

TOOLING

· Sharp Scissors
· Craft Glue
· Felting Needle

METHOD

1 THE NOSE

Using white yarn, wrap 10 times on the top half of your pom pom maker.

2 INNER NOSE

Using pink yarn, wrap 10 times covering half of the white nose, as shown.

3 OVER NOSE

With white, wrap over the pink 30 wraps, to make 2 layers.

4 FACE

Grey. Wrap the whole length of the pom pom maker 150 wraps.

5 EYES

Black, 12 wraps.

6 REST OF THE FACE

Grey. Wrap the top half of the pom pom maker until full (80-100 wraps).

7 EARS

Grey.
Wrap over your finger. Wrap 15 times.

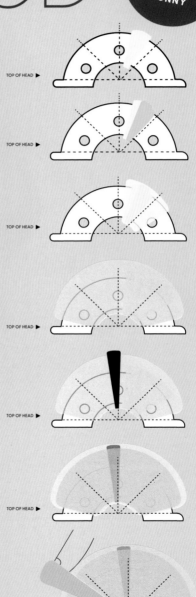

8 SECOND HALF

Using grey, wrap the bottom half of the pom pom maker until full (250 wraps).

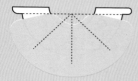

BRING IT TOGETHER

Bring the two halves of the pom pom maker together and join using the clip.

STEPS FOR CUTTING AND TYING

CUTTING

Hold the closed maker together and turn to the side. Use small, sharp scissors to cut in-between each side of the maker, as shown.

TYING

Use your waxed thread and wrap around the centre twice, before tying and pulling a tight knot. To be fully secure repeat with a second knot.

TRIMMING

Once you have your scissors, begin trimming your rabbit pom pom into shape, as shown in diagram 1. Pay careful attention to the curve of the head and cheeks.

We recommend you start by cutting into the eyes, following the diagram, to really accentuate the nose.

1 THE EYES

Trim around the eyes as shown. You will need to shorten the pom pom in this area to form the face, making sure to keep the nose longer.

2 THE HEAD

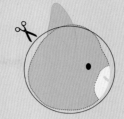

Shape the head as shown in the diagram. Do not cut the ears at this stage. focusing on the pear shaped curve around the top of the head.

3 THE NOSE

Cut at the areas 1,2 and 3 slowly, revealing the pink inner parts of the nose.

Lastly, continue trimming and neatening until you get the desired look.

NEEDLE FELTING

EYES AND EARS

Needle felt the black eyes until they are rounded. Once happy, you can stick your plastic eyes, then needle felt the ears and pink nose into a Y.

MAKES 1

50 MINS PER MAKE

PENELOPE THE PANDA

PANDA

YOU WILL NEED

- Pom Pom Maker (Medium)
- White or Cream Yarn
- Black Yarn
- Plastic Eyes (optional)
- Waxed Thread

TOOLING

- Sharp Scissors
- Craft Glue
- Felting Needle

19

METHOD

1 THE NOSE

Using black yarn, wrap 10 times on the top half of your pom pom maker.

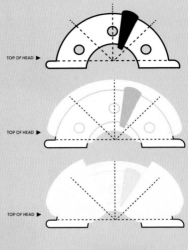

TOP OF HEAD ▶

2 THE HEAD

Using white or cream, wrap the full length of the pom pom maker, 3 layers (40 wraps).

TOP OF HEAD ▶

3 THE HEAD

White or cream.
Wrap each side 35 times, leaving the middle clear.

TOP OF HEAD ▶

4 EYES

Using black, wrap the centre part 30 wraps.

TOP OF HEAD ▶

5 THE HEAD

White or cream. Wrap the top half of the pom pom maker until full (100 wraps).

TOP OF HEAD ▶

6 EARS

Black. Wrap over your finger 15 wraps.

STEPS FOR THE BOTTOM HALF

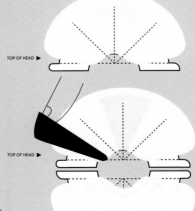

TOP OF HEAD ▶

6 SECOND HALF

Making sure you are on the bottom half of the maker, begin to wrap the cream or white yarn from left to right until it is fully covered. Around 250 wraps.

20

BRING IT TOGETHER

Bring the two halves of the pom pom maker together and join using the clip.

STEPS FOR CUTTING AND TYING

CUTTING

Hold the closed maker together and turn to the side. Use small, sharp scissors to cut in-between each side of the maker, as shown.

TYING

Use your waxed thread and wrap around the centre twice, before tying and pulling a tight knot. To be fully secure repeat with a second knot.

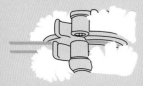

TRIMMING

Once you have your scissors, begin trimming your panda pom pom into shape, as shown in diagram 1. Pay careful attention to the curve of the nose and cheeks.

We recommend you start by cutting into the eyes, following the diagram, to really accentuate the nose.

1 THE EYES

Trim around the eyes as shown. You will need to shorten the pom pom in this area to form the face, making sure to keep the nose longer.

2 THE HEAD

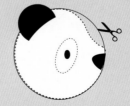

Shape the head as shown in the diagram. Do not cut the ears at this stage.

3 THE SIDE

Cut at the side angle to get the shape shown – particularly focusing on the curve around the nose and eyes.

Lastly, continue trimming and neatening until you get the desired look for your pom pom animal. Keep turning to check the animals shape looks right from all sides.

NEEDLE FELTING

Eyes

Needle felt the black yarn (the eyes) until they are rounded and stay in place. Once happy, you can stick your plastic eyes, on top of the yarn with craft glue.

Ears

For each ear, hold the yarn together before slowly needle felting. Do this until the ear stays in shape and the yarn is bonded. Then, cut into a rounded ear shape as shown below.

MAKES 1   50 MINS
PER MAKE

LEO
THE LION

THE LION

YOU WILL NEED

- Pom Pom Maker (Medium)
- Golden Brown Yarn
- Light Brown Yarn
- White Yarn
- Black Yarn
- Plastic Eyes (yellow)
- Waxed Thread
- Card

TOOLING

- Sharp Scissors
- Craft Glue
- Felting Needle

METHOD

1 THE NOSE
Using black yarn, 8 wraps.

2 THE FACE
Using light brown, wrap the left side of the pom pom 60 wraps.

3 THE MUZZLE
White. Wrap next to black 30 wraps.

4 EYES
Using white, wrap a small section halfway across the light brown face, 10 wraps.

5 THE FACE
Light brown.
Wrap the top half of the pom pom maker until full. 80 wraps.

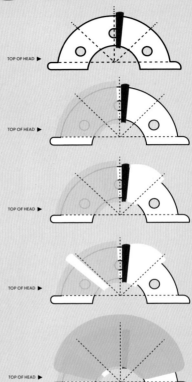

STEPS FOR THE SECOND HALF

SECOND HALF - THE LIONS MANE

You will need a piece of cardboard 5" X 3". Cut two slits on either side, as per the image.
Now wrap your golden brown yarn around the cardboard, so the cut lines are on the right and left (100 wraps).
Take your pom pom and place it in the centre of your cardboard. Then, tie the wax thread through the two slits you cut out earlier. Make a double knot. Rip the top of the cardboard. Pull the wax thread tight and make a single knot. Remove the bottom half of the cardboard.

Cut the loop you have created (top and bottom). You should start to see your lion begin to take shape.
Start needle felting the back of the mane to form a pom pom shape. Joining the pieces together.

Then you can now start cutting your lion into shape.

STEPS FOR CUTTING AND TYING

CUTTING

Hold the closed maker together and turn to the side. Use small, sharp scissors to cut in-between each side of the maker, as shown.

TYING

Use your waxed thread and wrap around the centre twice, before tying and pulling a tight knot. To be fully secure repeat with a second knot.

TRIMMING

Once you have your scissors, begin trimming your lion pom pom into shape, as shown in diagram 1. Pay careful attention to the curve of the nose and cheeks.

We recommend you start by cutting into the eyes, following the diagram, to really accentuate the nose.

1 THE EYES

Trim around the eyes as shown. You will need to shorten the pom pom in this area to form the face, making sure to keep the nose longer.

2 THE HEAD

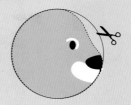

Shape the head as shown in the diagram.

3 THE SIDE

Cut at the side angle to get the shape shown – particularly focusing on the curve around the nose and eyes.

Lastly, continue trimming and neatening until you get the desired look for your pom pom animal. Keep turning to check the animals shape looks right from all sides.

NEEDLE FELTING

Eyes

Needle felt the white yarn (the eyes) until they are rounded and stay in place. Once happy, you can stick your plastic eyes, on top of the yarn with craft glue.

MAKES 1

35 MINS PER MAKE

POPPY THE POODLE

26

POODLE

THIS IS AN EASIER PROJECT TO TRY WHEN YOU ARE FIRST LEARNING POM POM ANIMALS!

YOU WILL NEED

· Pom Pom Maker (Medium)
· White, Beige or Black Poodle Yarn (depending on the colour of poodle you want to make)
· Plastic Eyes & Nose
· Waxed Thread

TOOLING

· Sharp Scissors
· Craft Glue
· Sewing Needle

27

METHOD

1 THE HEAD

White.
Wrap 120 times around the top half of the pom pom maker.

TOP OF HEAD ▶

STEPS FOR THE SECOND HALF

2 THE SECOND HALF

White.
Wrap 120 times around the bottom of the pom pom maker.

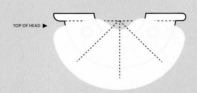

TOP OF HEAD ▶

BRING IT TOGETHER

Bring the two halves of the pom pom maker together and join using the clip.

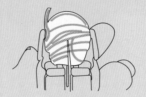

TYING

Use your waxed thread and wrap around the centre twice, before tying and pulling a tight knot. To be fully secure repeat with a second knot.

THE NEXT STEP

The next step is to make the ears, you will need to make two more, slightly smaller, pom poms. Follow the same process but this time only wrap 65 times and do not cut the waxed thread after tying.

STEPS FOR CUTTING AND TYING

CUTTING

Hold the closed maker together and turn to the side. Use small, sharp scissors to cut in-between each side of the maker, as shown.

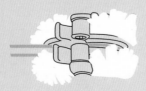

28

ATTACH THE EARS

To attach the ears, thread the waxed thread from one small pom pom through a sewing needle (1). Feed it through the large pom pom and leave the thread loose on the other side (2). Now, you can tie the loose thread to the waxed thread on the second small pom pom (3). These will form the ears so when in the right place, pull tight and tie together.

TRIMMING

Once you have your scissors, begin trimming your dog pom pom into shape, as shown in diagram 1.

We recommend you start by cutting into the eyes, following the diagram, to really accentuate the nose.

1 THE EYES

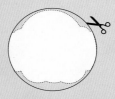

Trim around the eyes as shown. You will need to shorten the pom pom in this area to form the face, making sure to keep the nose bigger.

2 THE NEXT STEP

The next step is to attach the eyes and nose. These should just push into place. You can also glue these if you want to ensure they don't fall out. But we suggest you do this at the end so you are certain they are in the right position.

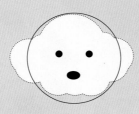

3 THE HEAD

Shape the head as shown in the diagram.

3 THE EARS

For each ear, cut into a rounded ear shape as shown below, this only requires a little shaping.

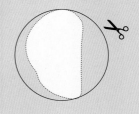

TRY IN OTHER COLOURS TO MAKE MORE POODLES!

BERTIE
THE BUDGIE

BUDGIE

YOU WILL NEED

- Pom Pom Maker (Medium)
- Dark Blue Yarn
- White Yarn
- Black Yarn
- Yellow Felting Wool
- Plastic Eyes (optional)
- Waxed thread

TOOLING

- Felting Needle
- Craft Glue
- Sharp Scissors

METHOD

1 HEAD

Using dark blue, wrap 11 times.

TOP OF HEAD ▶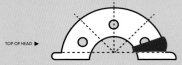

2 HEAD

White.
Wrap 60 times.

TOP OF HEAD ▶

3 HEAD MARKINGS

Black.
Wrap 6 times.

TOP OF HEAD ▶

4 HEAD

With white, wrap 70 times covering
the top half of the maker, leaving
the blue uncovered.

TOP OF HEAD ▶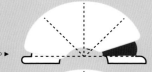

5 HEAD MARKINGS

Black.
Wrap 6 times.

TOP OF HEAD ▶

6 HEAD

Using white, wrap 70 times over the
whole top half of the pom pom maker.

TOP OF HEAD ▶

7 HEAD

Black.
Wrap 11 times.

TOP OF HEAD ▶

8 HEAD

Using white, wrap 110 times over the
whole top half of the pom pom maker.

TOP OF HEAD ▶

8 BODY

Dark Blue.
Wrap 250 times.

BRING IT TOGETHER

Bring the two halves
of the pom pom maker
together and join using
the clip.

STEPS FOR CUTTING AND TYING

CUTTING

Hold the closed maker
together and turn to the
side. Use small, sharp
scissors to cut in-between
each side of the maker, as
shown.

TYING

Use your waxed thread
and wrap around the
centre twice, before tying
and pulling a tight knot.
To be fully secure repeat
with a second knot.

TRIMMING

Once you have your
scissors, begin trimming
your budgie pom pom
into shape, as shown in
diagram 1. Pay careful
attention to the curve of
the nose and cheeks.

We recommend you start
by cutting into the eyes,
following the diagram,
to really accentuate the
nose.

1 THE EYES

Trim around the eyes as
shown. You will need to
shorten the pom pom in
this area to form the face,
making sure to keep the
nose longer.

2 THE HEAD

Shape the head as shown
in the diagram.

3 THE SIDE

Cut at the side angle to
get the shape shown –
particularly focusing on
the curve around the nose
and eyes.

Lastly, continue trimming
and neatening until you
get the desired look for
your pom pom animal.
Keep turning to check the
animals shape looks right
from all sides.

NEEDLE FELTING

Yellow Beak

Get a small piece of
yellow felting wool and
hold over the nose area.
Use your felting needle
to attach the yellow and
create a beak shape.
Followed by attaching
the eyes.

MAKES 1   45 MINS
            TO MAKE

HARRY THE HAMSTER

HAMSTER

YOU WILL NEED

· Pom Pom Maker (Medium)
· Golden Brown Yarn
· White Yarn
· Pink Yarn
· Plastic Eyes (optional)
· Waxed Thread

TOOLING

· Felting Needle
· Craft Glue
· Sharp Scissors

METHOD

1 INNER NOSE
Pink. Wrap 10 times.

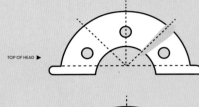

2 NOSE
White. Wrap 25 times.

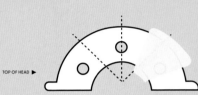

3 FACE
Golden Brown. Wrap 150 times.

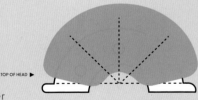

4 EARS
Golden Brown. 10 wraps over your finger 10 wraps.

STEPS FOR THE BOTTOM HALF

5 HEAD
Golden Brown.
Wrap 200 times.

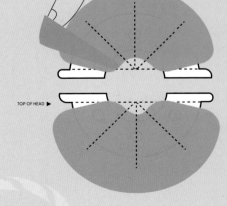

BRING IT TOGETHER

Bring the two halves of the pom pom maker together and join using the clip..

STEPS FOR CUTTING AND TYING

CUTTING

Hold the closed maker together and turn to the side. Use small, sharp scissors to cut in-between each side of the maker, as shown.

TYING

Use your wax thread and wrap around the centre twice, before tying and pulling a tight knot. To be fully secure repeat with a second knot.

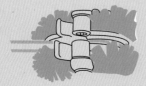

TRIMMING

Once you have your scissors, begin trimming your hamster pom pom into shape, as shown in diagram. Pay careful attention to the curve of the nose and cheeks.

We recommend you start by cutting into the eyes, following the diagram 1, accentuate the nose and cut into the cheeks for the best hamster shape.

1 THE EYES

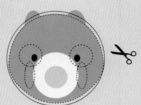

Trim around the eyes as shown. You will need to shorten the pom pom in this area to form the face, making sure to keep the nose longer.

2 THE HEAD

Shape the head as shown in the diagram. Do not cut the ears at this stage.

3 THE SIDE

Cut at the side angle to get the shape shown – particularly focusing on the curve around the nose and eyes.

Lastly, continue trimming and neatening until you get the desired look for your pom pom animal. Keep turning to check the animals shape looks right from all sides.

STICKING THE EYES

Once happy with shaping your hamster, you can stick your plastic eyes, provided in your kit, on top of the yarn with craft glue.

NEEDLE FELTING

Ears

For each ear, hold the yarn together before slowly needle felting. Do this until the ear stays in shape and the yarn is bonded. Then, cut into a small curved ear shape as shown in diagram 1.

MAKES
1

45 MINS
TO MAKE

SIMON
THE SLOTH

SLOTH

YOU WILL NEED

- Pom Pom Maker (Medium)
- Dark Brown Yarn
- White Yarn
- Golden Brown Yarn
- Plastic Eyes (optional)
- Waxed Thread

TOOLING

- Felting Needle
- Craft Glue
- Sharp Scissors

METHOD

1 INNER NOSE
Using dark brown yarn, wrap 10 times.

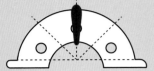

2 NOSE
Golden Brown. Wrap 15 times over the dark brown

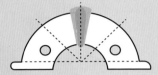

3 FACE
White Yarn. Wrap 40 times evenly over the nose and remaining section.

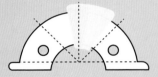

4 EYES
Dark Brown Yarn.
Wrap 25 times, overlapping a small section of the white yarn.

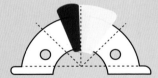

5 FACE
Using white, wrap 30 times over the dark brown eyes.

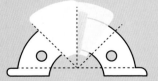

6 HEAD
Golden Brown.
Wrap 70 times each side, leaving a gap in the centre.

8 SECOND HALF

Golden Brown Yarn. Wrap 150 – 200 times.

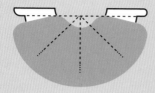

BRING IT TOGETHER

Bring the two halves of the pom pom maker together and join using the clip.

STEPS FOR CUTTING AND TYING

CUTTING

Hold the closed maker together and turn to the side. Use small, sharp scissors to cut in-between each side of the maker, as shown.

TYING

Use your waxed thread and wrap around the centre twice, before tying and pulling a tight knot. To be fully secure repeat with a second knot.

TRIMMING

Once you have your scissors, begin trimming your sloth pom pom into shape, as shown in diagram 1. Pay careful attention to the curve of the head and cheeks.

We recommend you start by cutting into the eyes, following the diagram, to really accentuate the nose.

1 THE EYES

Trim around the eyes as shown. You will need to shorten the pom pom in this area to form the face, making sure to keep the nose longer.

2 THE HEAD

Shape the head as shown in the diagram.

Lastly stick on the Sloth's eyes.

MAKES 1

50 MINS TO MAKE

SAMMY THE SEAL

42

SEAL

YOU WILL NEED

· Pom Pom Maker (Medium)
· Blue or Grey Yarn
· White Yarn
· White Felting Wool
· Plastic Eyes & Nose
· Waxed Thread
· Felt Sheets

TOOLING

· Felting Needle
· Craft Glue
· Sharp Scissors
· Marker Pen

METHOD

1 UNDER BODY

With white yarn, wrap the top half of the pom pom maker until full (90 wraps).

2 UNDER BODY

Blue Yarn. Wrap the top half of the pom pom maker until full (120 wraps).

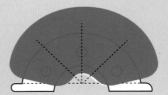

STEPS FOR THE BOTTOM HALF

3 HEAD / FACE

Blue Yarn. Wrap the bottom half of the pom pom maker until full (200 wraps). and remaining section.

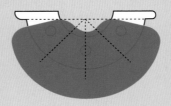

BRING IT TOGETHER

Bring the two halves of the pom pom maker together and join using the clip. wrap on the 'top of head'.

STEPS FOR CUTTING AND TYING

CUTTING

Hold the closed maker together and turn to the side. Use small, sharp scissors to cut in-between each side of the maker, as shown.

TYING

Use your wax thread and wrap around the centre twice, before tying and pulling a tight knot. To be fully secure repeat with a second knot.

TRIMMING

Once you have your scissors, begin trimming your seal pom pom into a rounded shape, .

1. ADD THE WHITE SNOUT

Get a small piece of white felting wool and hold over the nose area. Poke your felting needle to attach the white and create cheeks.

Use a black marker to draw 3 dots on each check for whiskers.

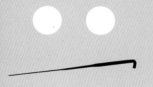

2 ADD THE EYES

Once happy, you can stick your plastic eyes on with craft glue.

3 FLIPPERS

To make the flippers, you want to use a piece of felt, cut into two and place one on top of each other. With a pencil, lightly draw the shape we have provided (3. Flippers).
Now, with a sharp pair of scissors, cut around the shape. This will leave you with two flippers. Once cut out, glue these in place.with craft glue.

4 TAIL

To make the tail,follow the same ,etjpd as the flippers and lightly draw the shape we have provided and cut out (4. Tail).
Once cut out, glue this in place with craft glue.

5 SEAL TWO

Repeat the steps to create the next seal, using different coloured yarn.

BUNNY GARLAND

YOU WILL NEED

· Pom Pom Maker (Medium)
· Grey, Dark Grey and Brown Yarn (For Bunnies)
· White Yarn
· Pink Yarn
· Yarn in your chosen colours for your plain pom poms in the garland
· Plastic Eyes (optional)
· Waxed Thread

TOOLING

· Felting Needle
· Craft Glue
· Sharp Scissors
· Sewing Needle

METHOD

REPEAT STEPS UNTIL YOU HAVE 3 BUNNIES FOR THE GARLAND!

MAKE YOUR BUNNIES

Repeat all the required steps from the "rabbit" pom pom make, trimming each bunny until shaped and needle felting where required. We recommend you pre-make at least 3 bunnies for your garland. We choose to do these in light grey, dark grey and beige yarn. However it is up to you which colours you use, so get creative and make them in any colour you wish!

IMPORTANT:

When tieing the bunnies - instead of cutting the waxed thread as you did in the other makes, in this project you will need to keep the waxed thread long so you can use this later when tieing all your bunnies inot the garland.

Remember, do not cut the string after tying each pom pom.

EYES, EARS AND NOSE

Needle felt your bunnies as you did in the "rabbit" make. Needle felt the black yarn (the eyes) until they are rounded. Cut and needle felt the pink nose as you did in the first "rabbit" make. Once happy, you can add plastic eyes, then needle felt and cut the ears.

MAKING PLAIN POM POMS

To decorate your garland, you will need a selection of plain pom poms between your bunnies. We recommend alternating one bunny then one plain pom pom, but you can always do more!

To make a plain pom pom simply wrap your pom pom maker with your chosen yarn colour (purple and green is what we have chosen for ours). Wrap both sides of the pom pom maker (top and bottom). The more wraps you do the fluffier the pom poms will be.

Once done, cut and remove from your pom pom maker, as you did in the other projects.

FINAL TOUCHES

Once you have finished. You just need to tie each pom pom (using the uncut waxed thread we left on each) to a long piece of yarn. Join in a chain. You can make this as long, or short, as you like!